Spectacular Uses for a
SAGGY SCR

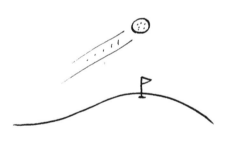

ALLAN PLENDERLEITH

ℛ
RAVETTE PUBLISHING

Published by Ravette Publishing Limited.
PO Box 876, Horsham, West Sussex RH12 9GH

ISBN: 978-1-84161-335-2

For more cartoons and exclusive merchandise visit
www.allanplenderleith.com

For David and Susan.

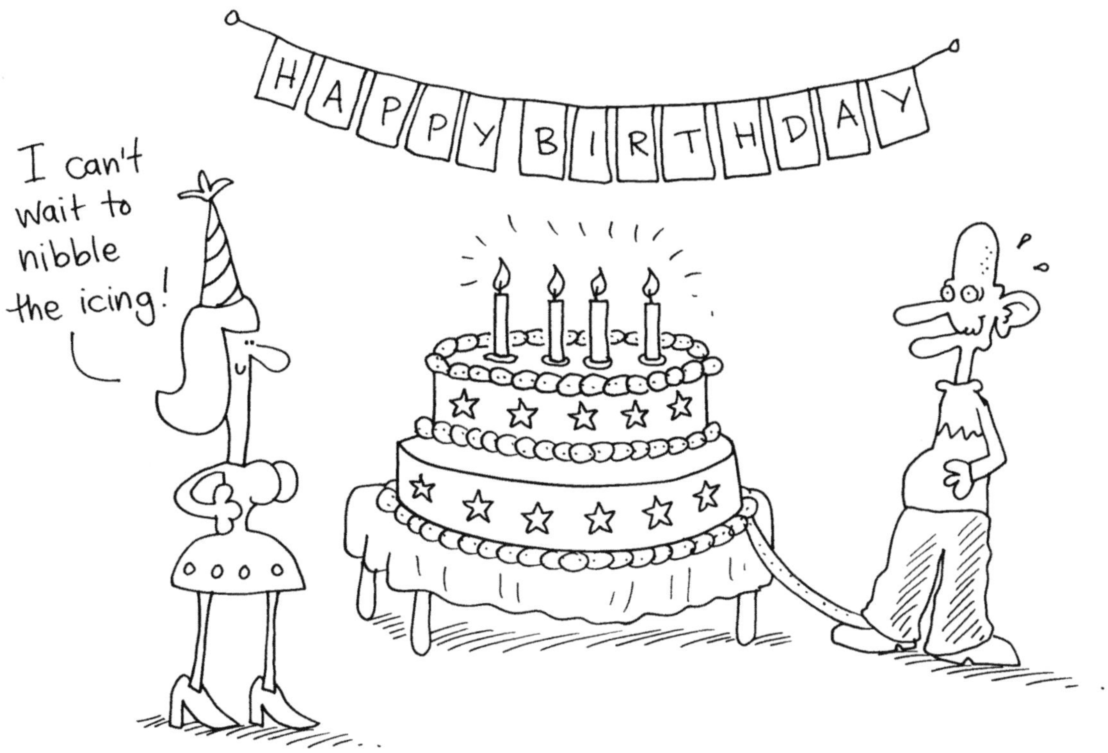
HAPPY BIRTHDAY
I can't wait to nibble the icing!

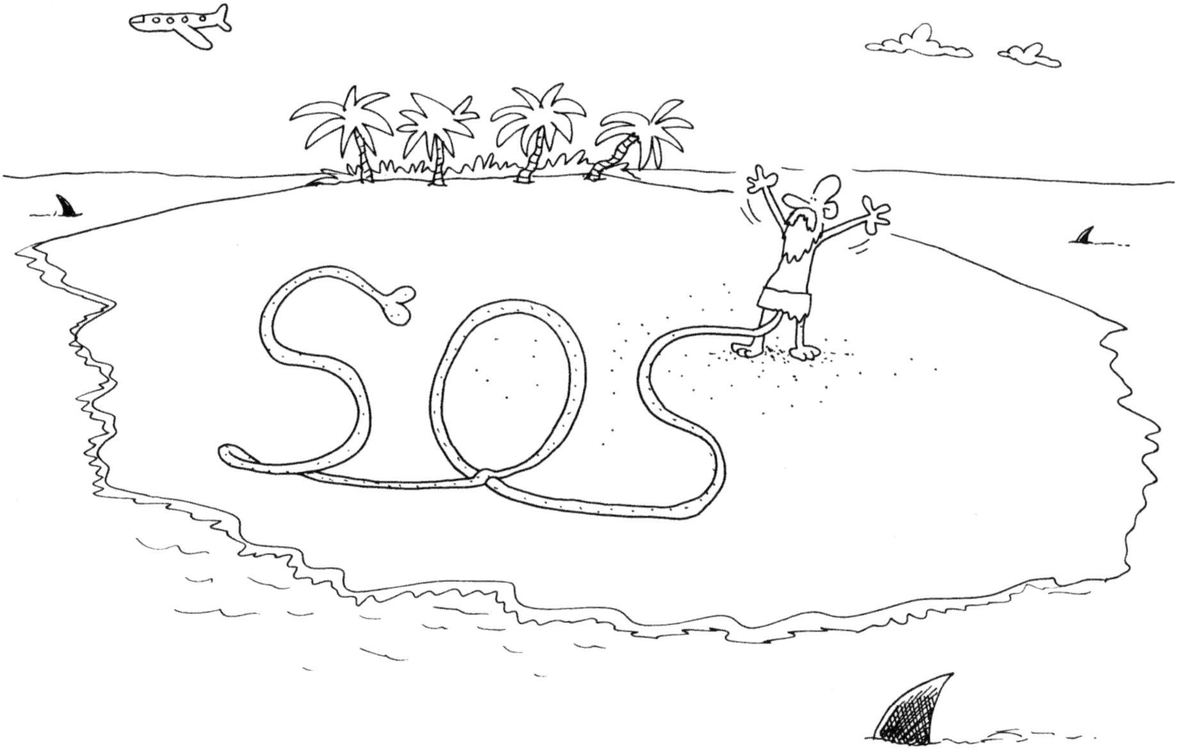
SOS

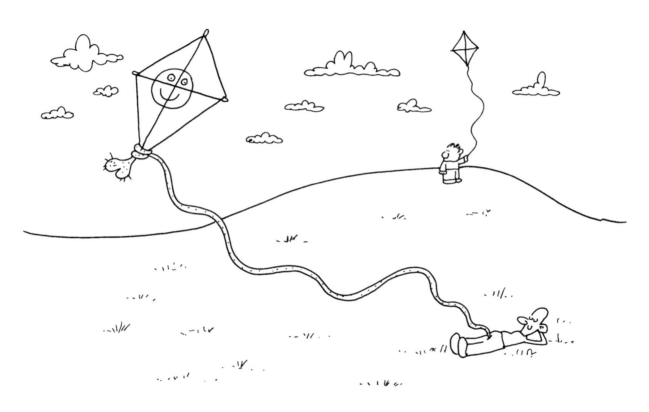

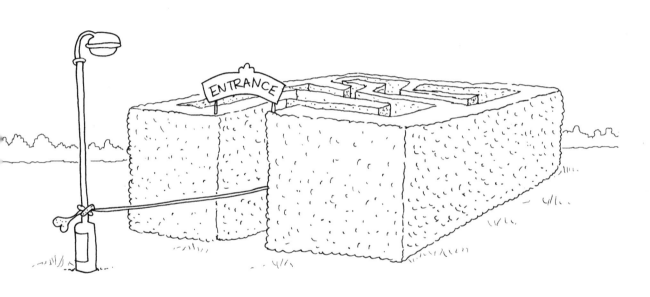

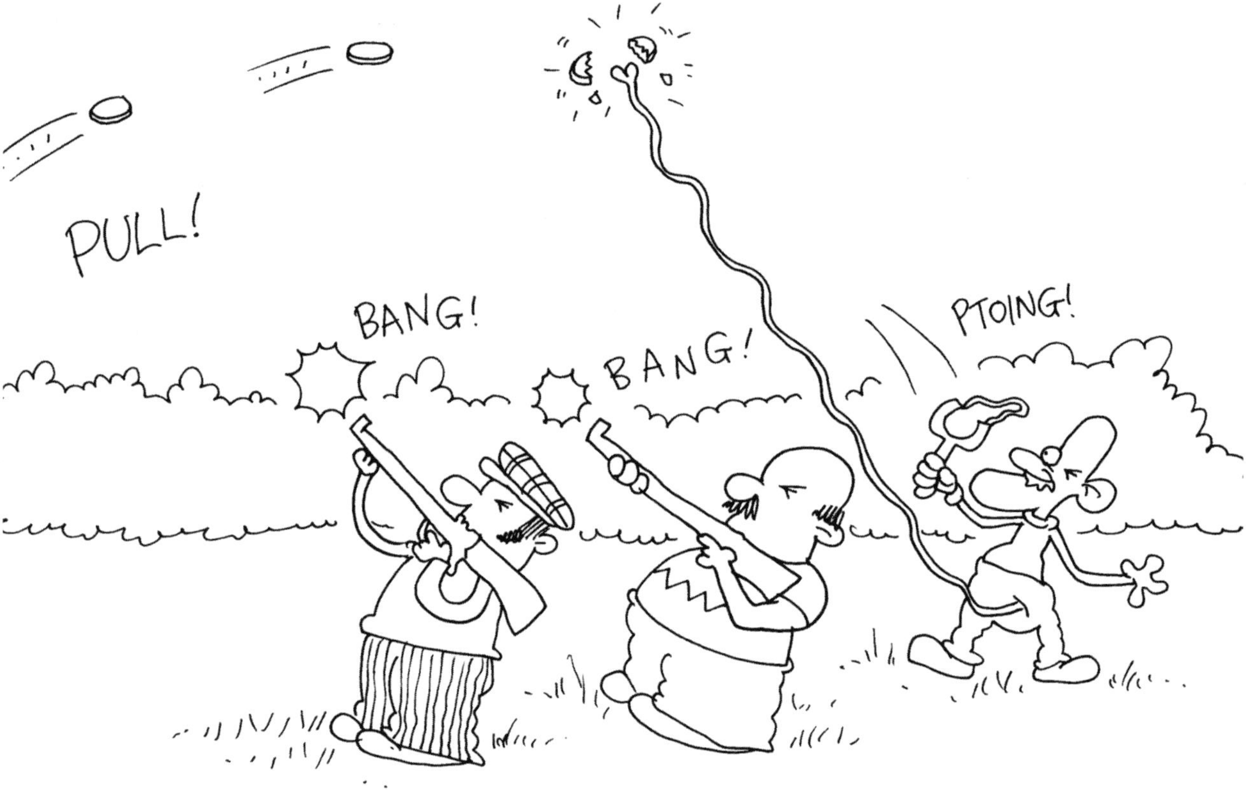
PULL!
BANG!
BANG!
PTOING!